The Rude Cursing Designs

SWEARY

COLORING BOOK FOR ADULTS

Swear Word Coloring Book

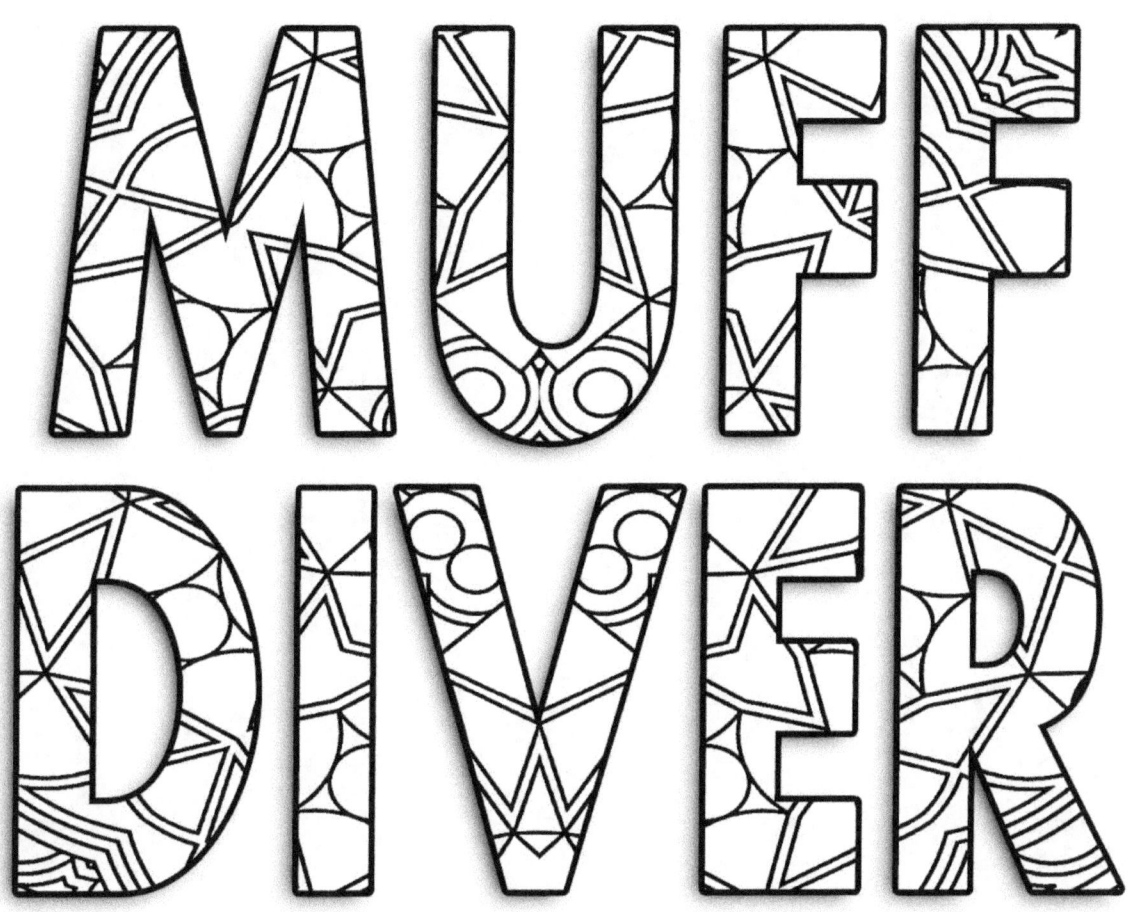

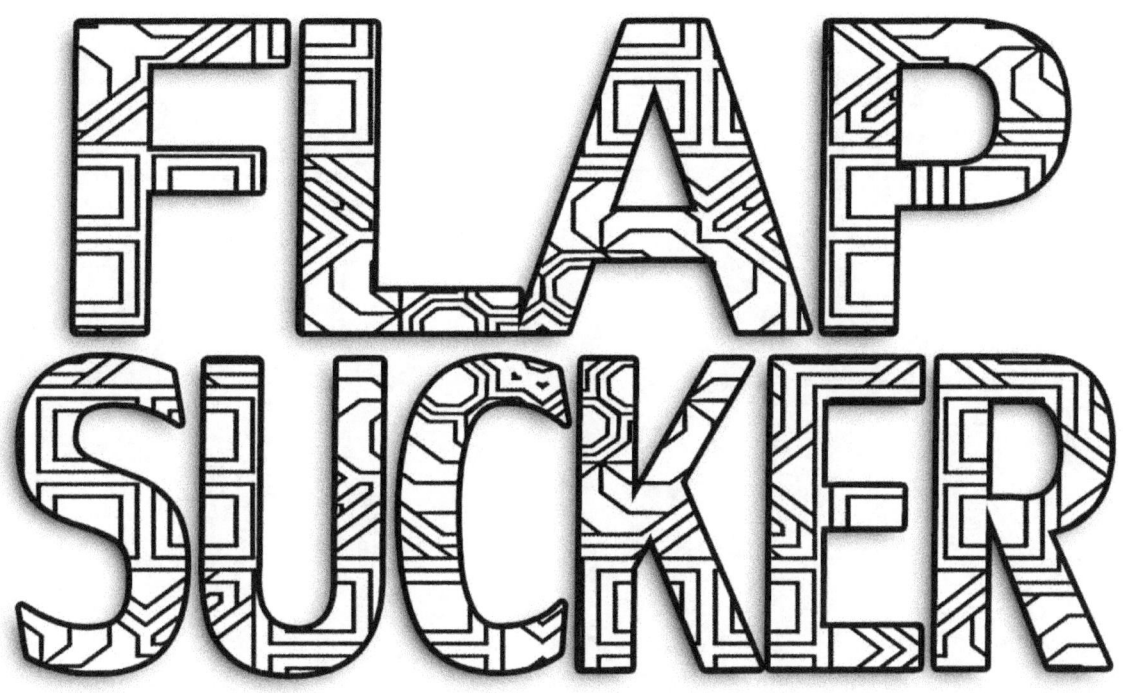

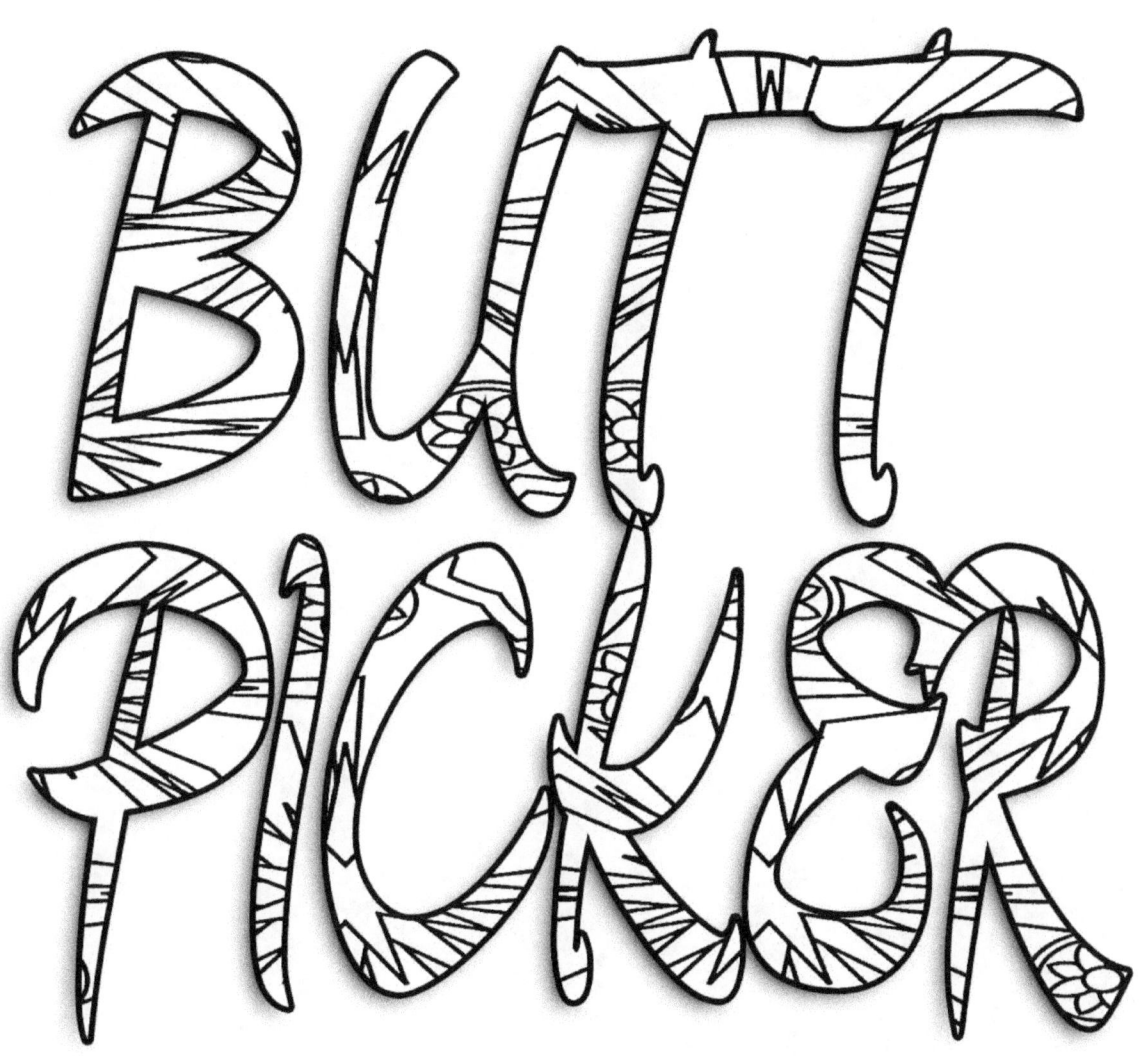

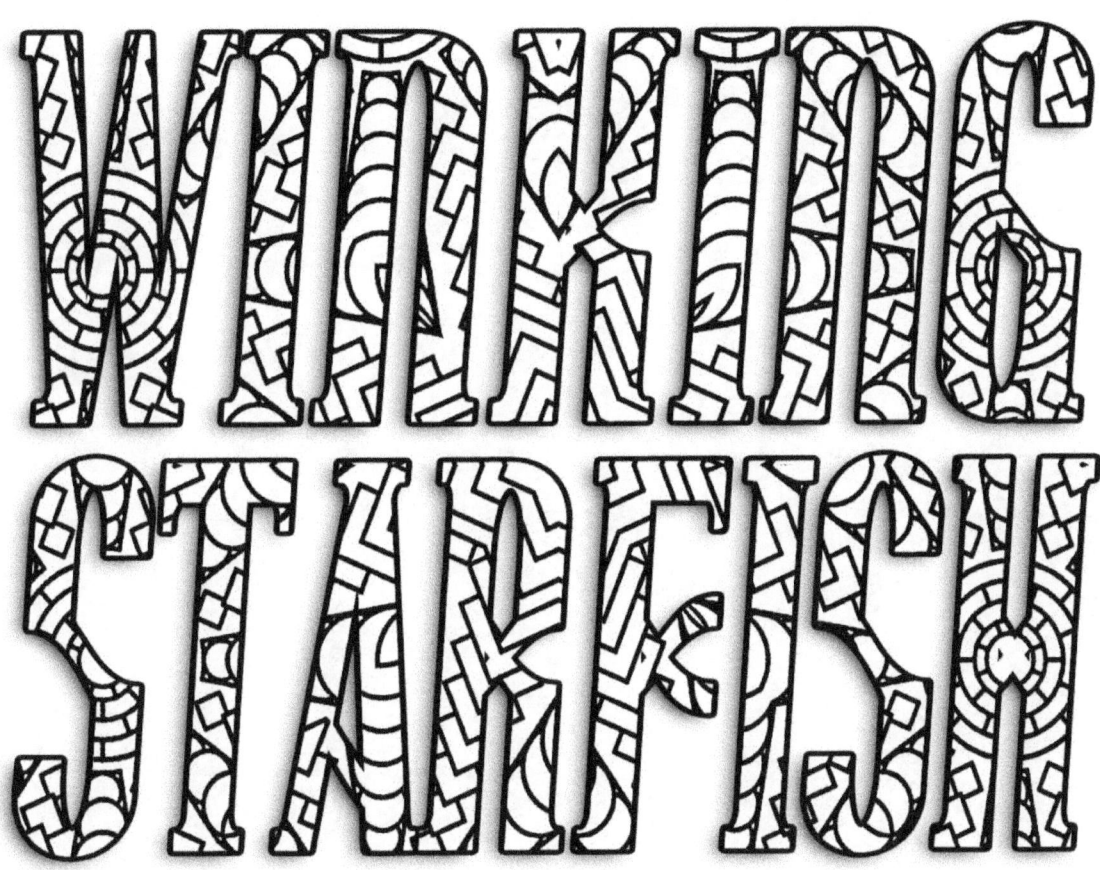

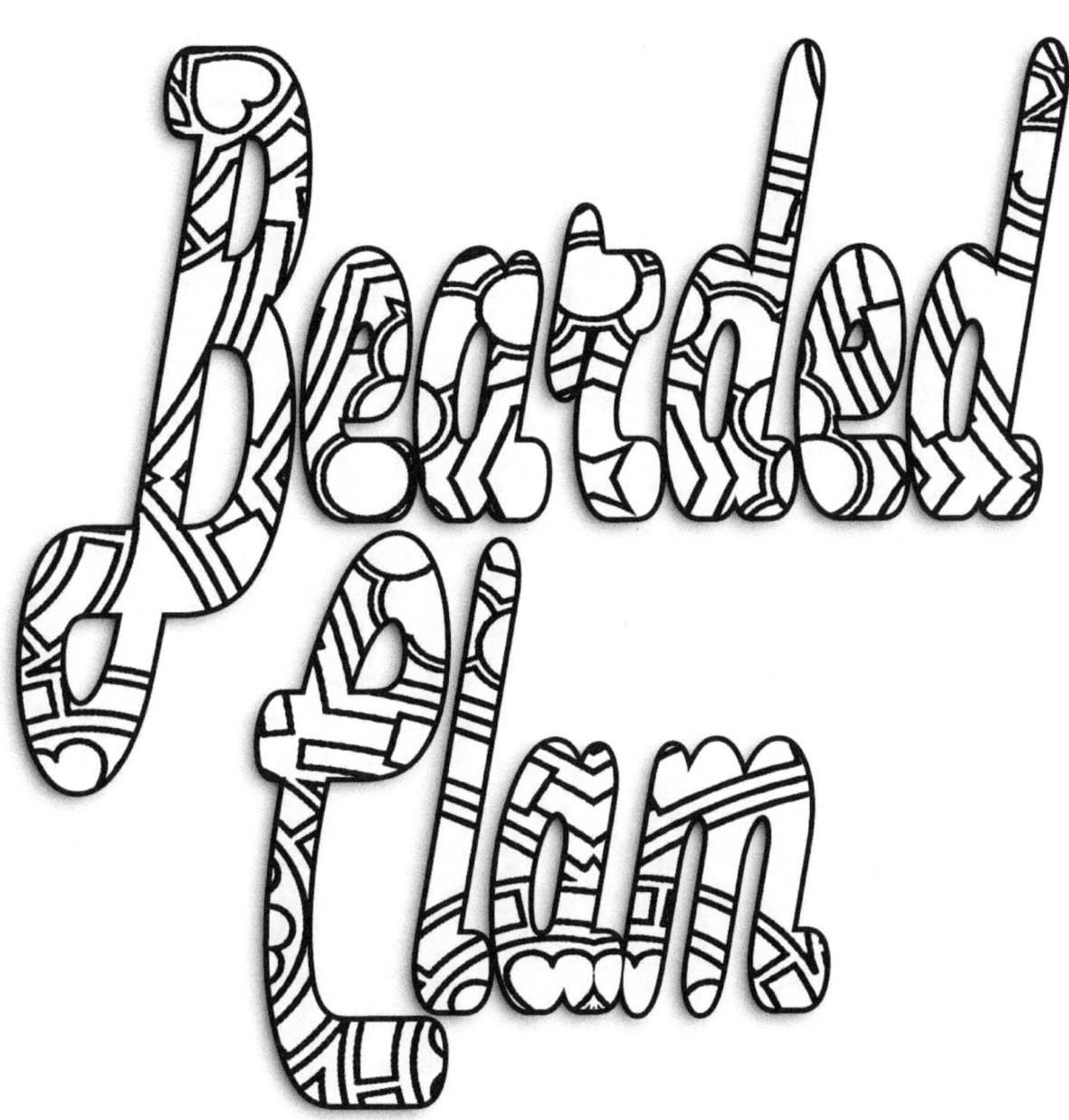

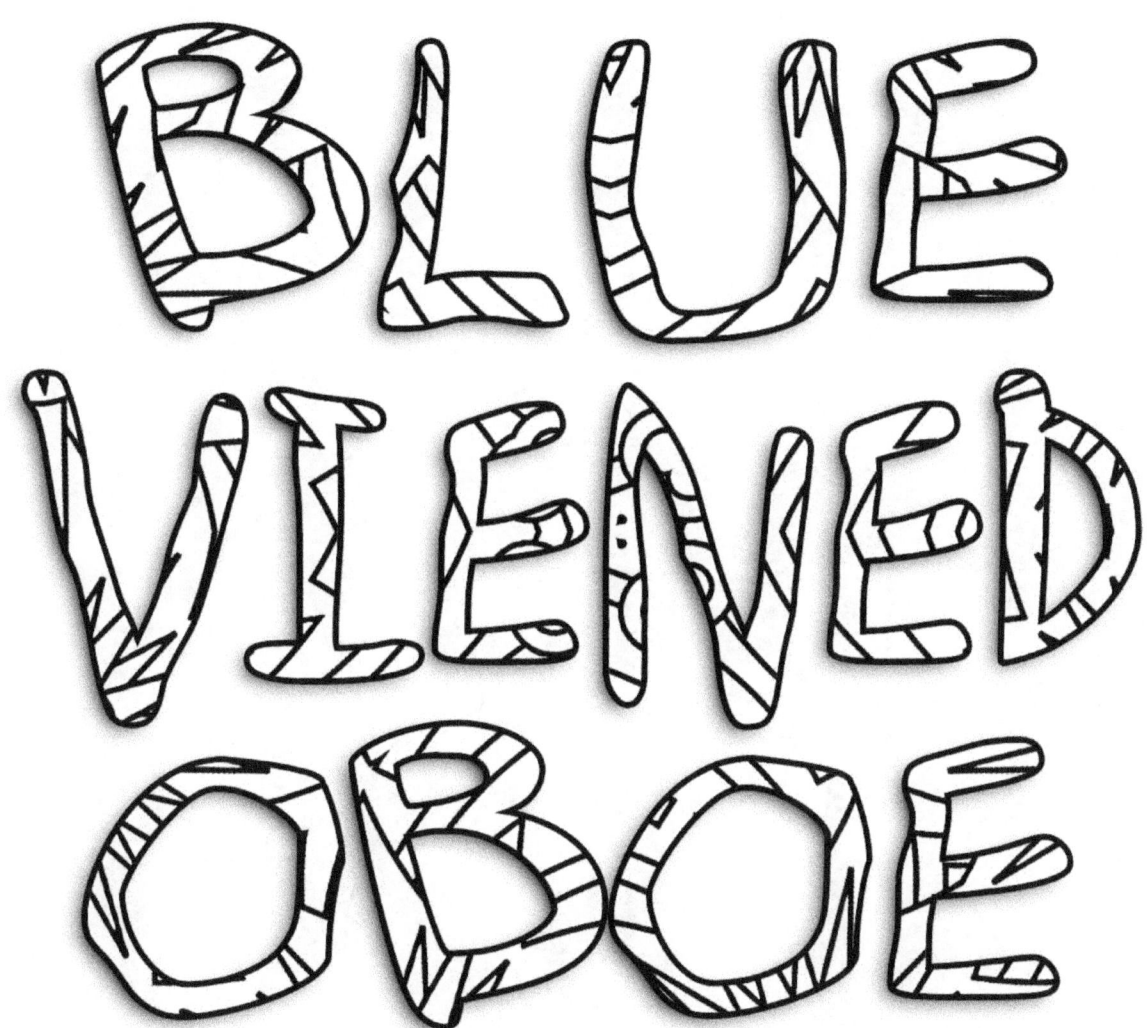

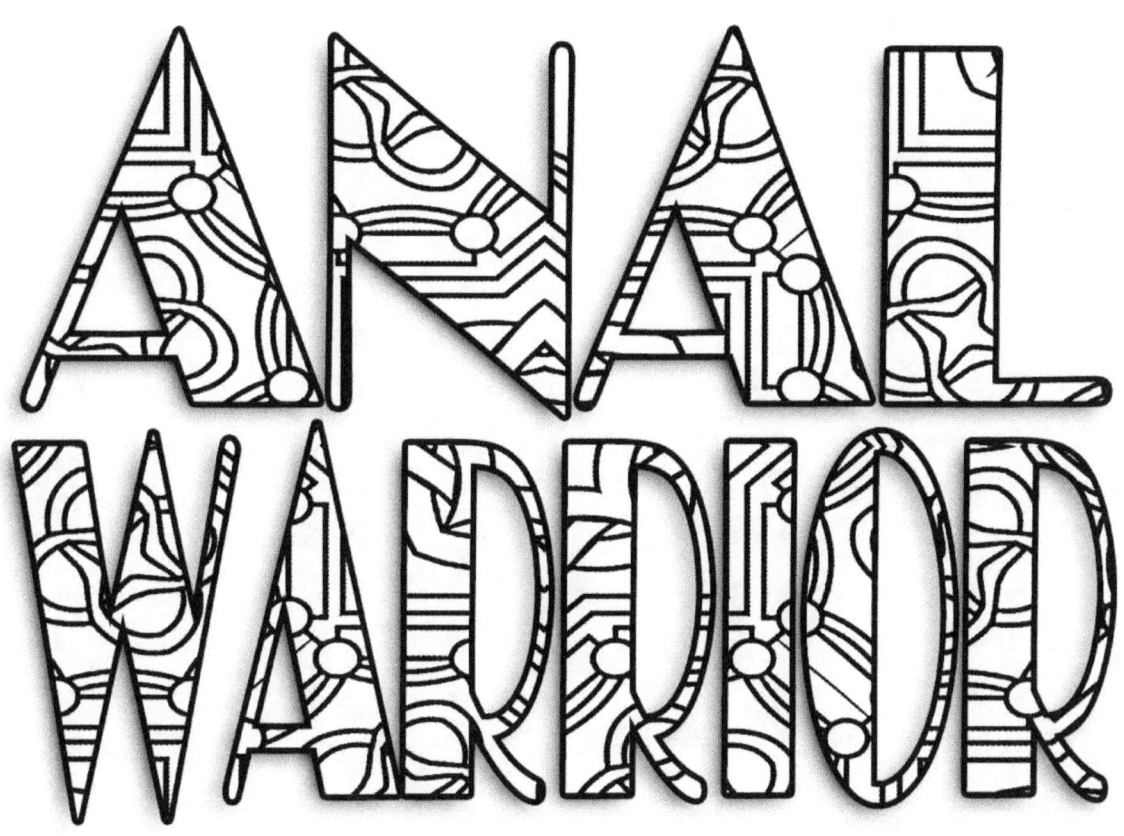

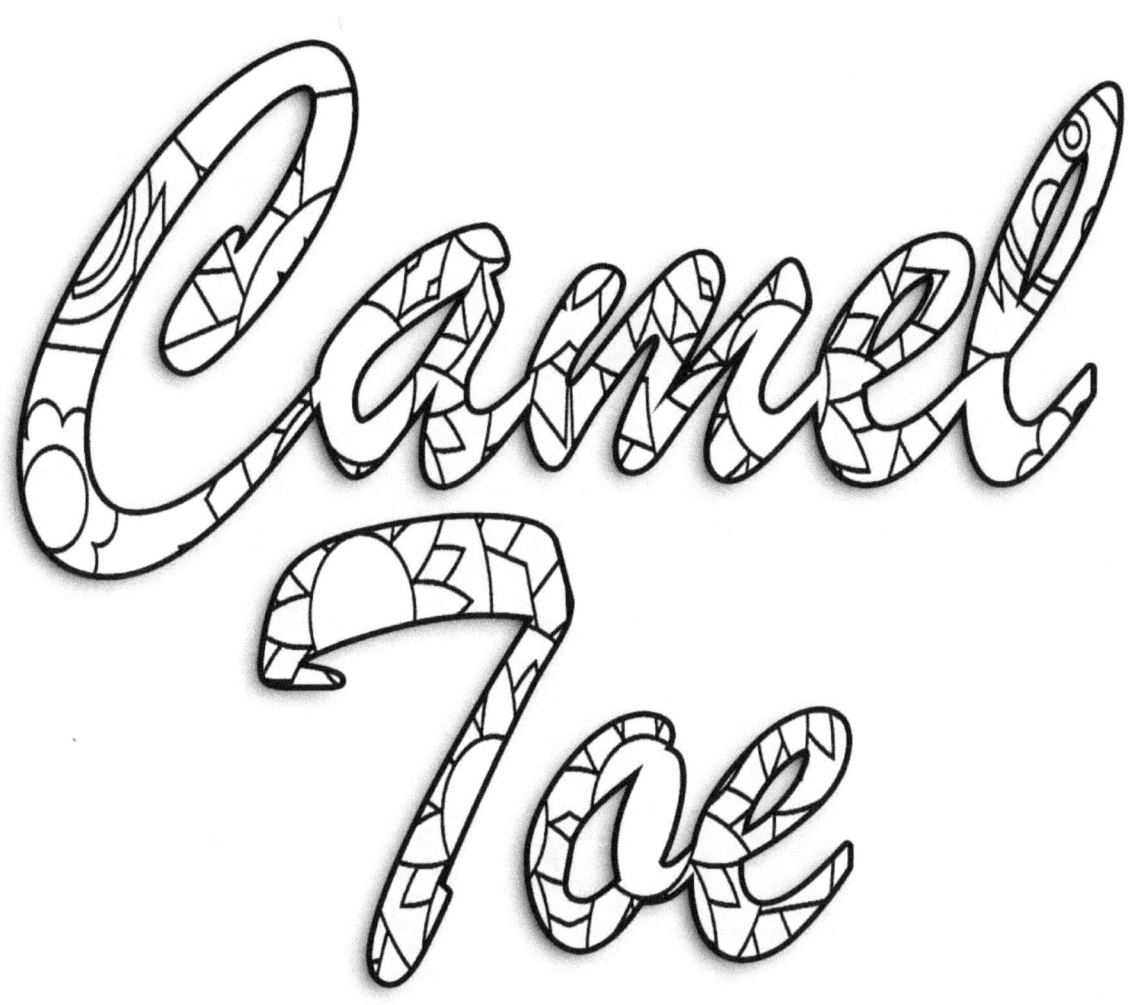

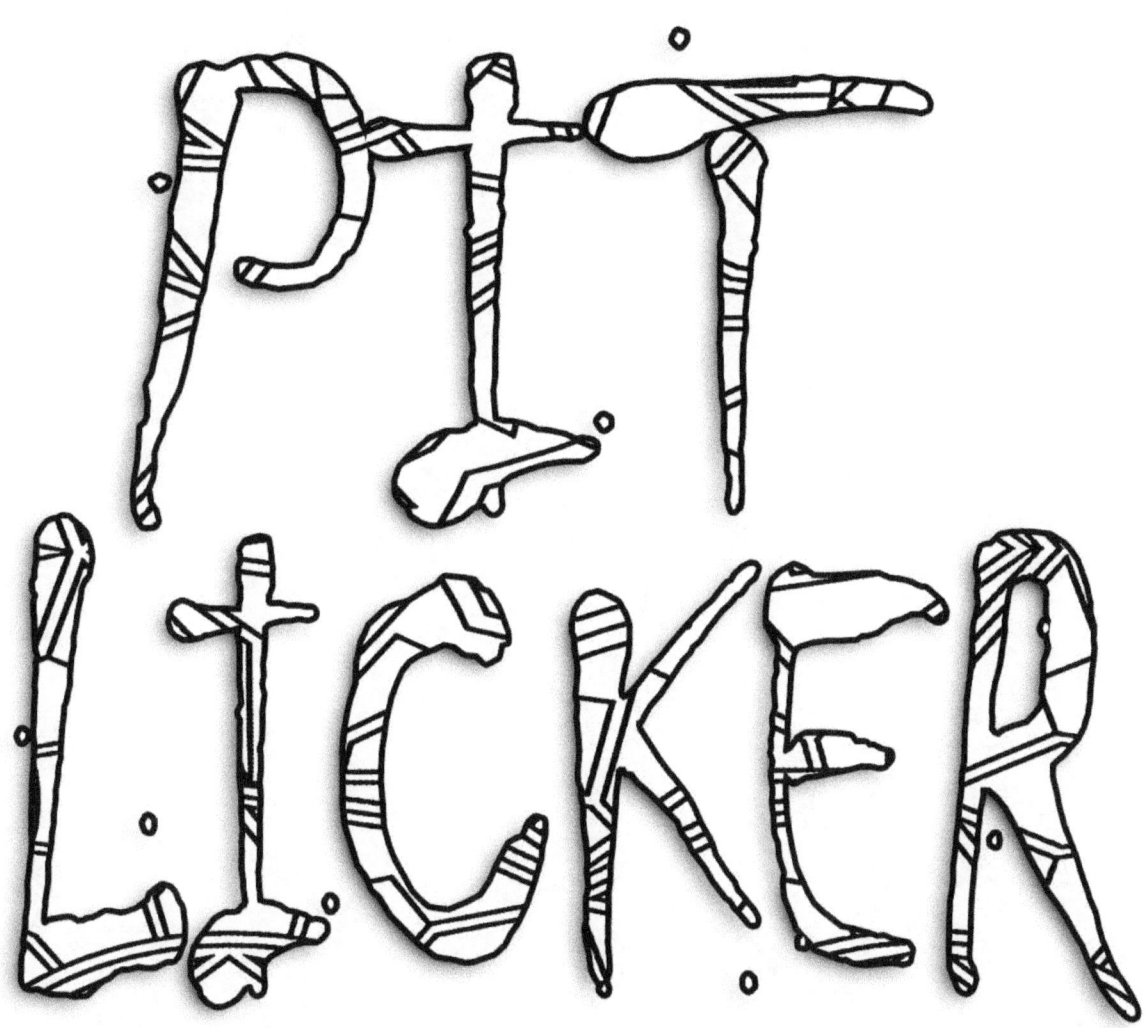

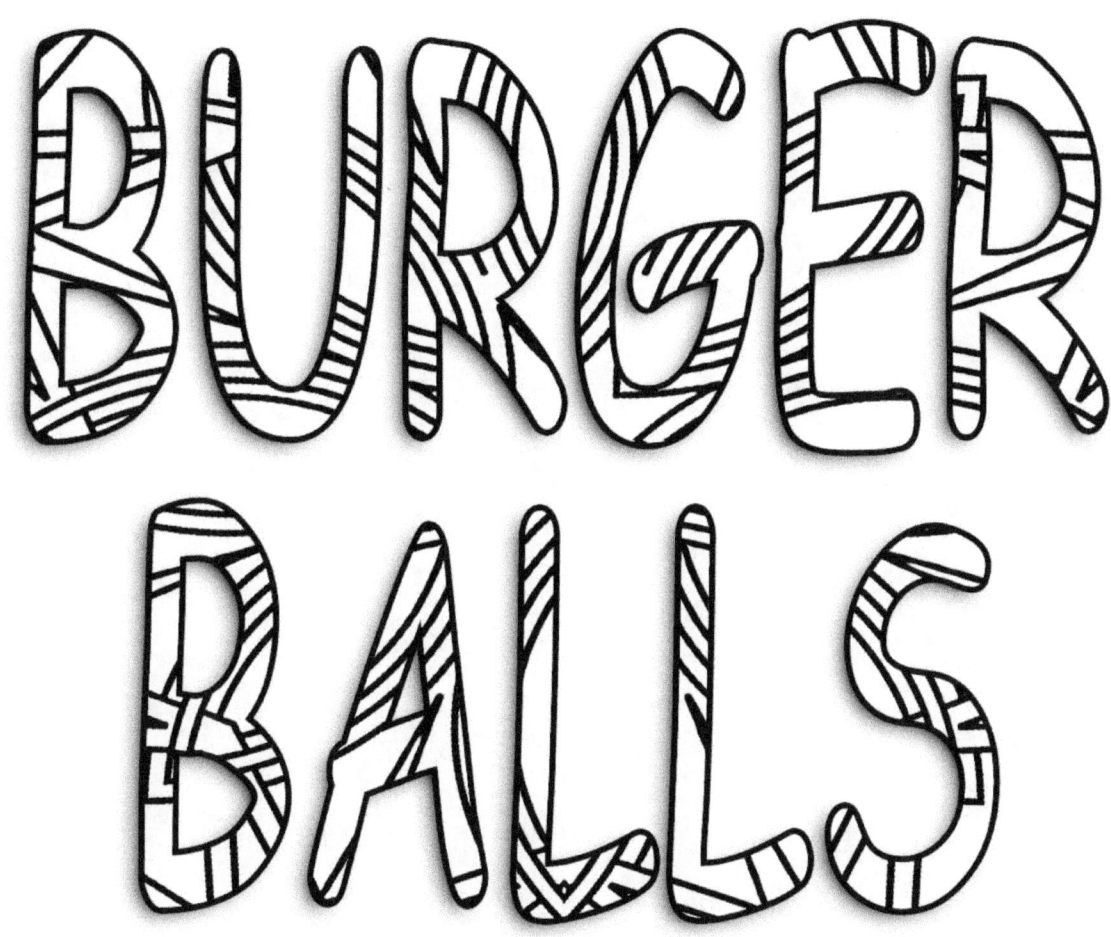

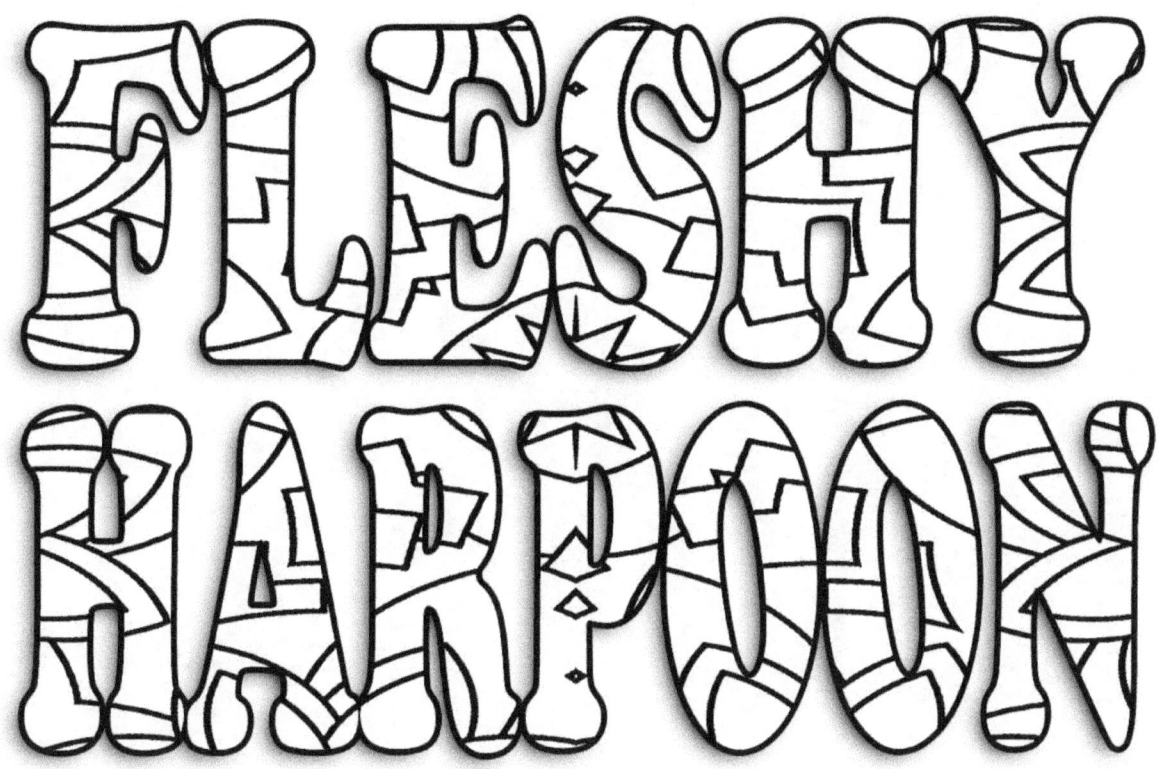

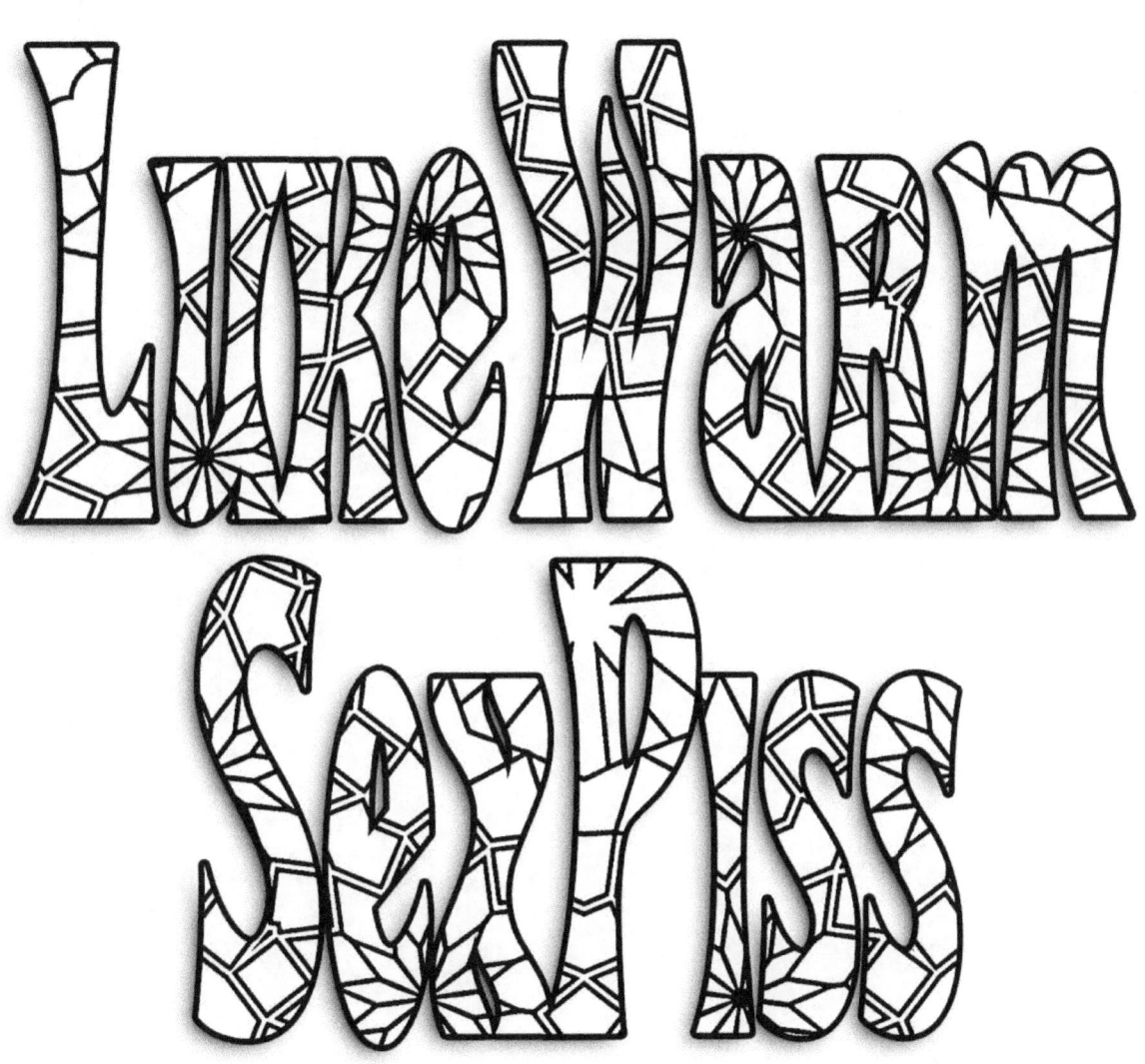

SLICK SNATCH

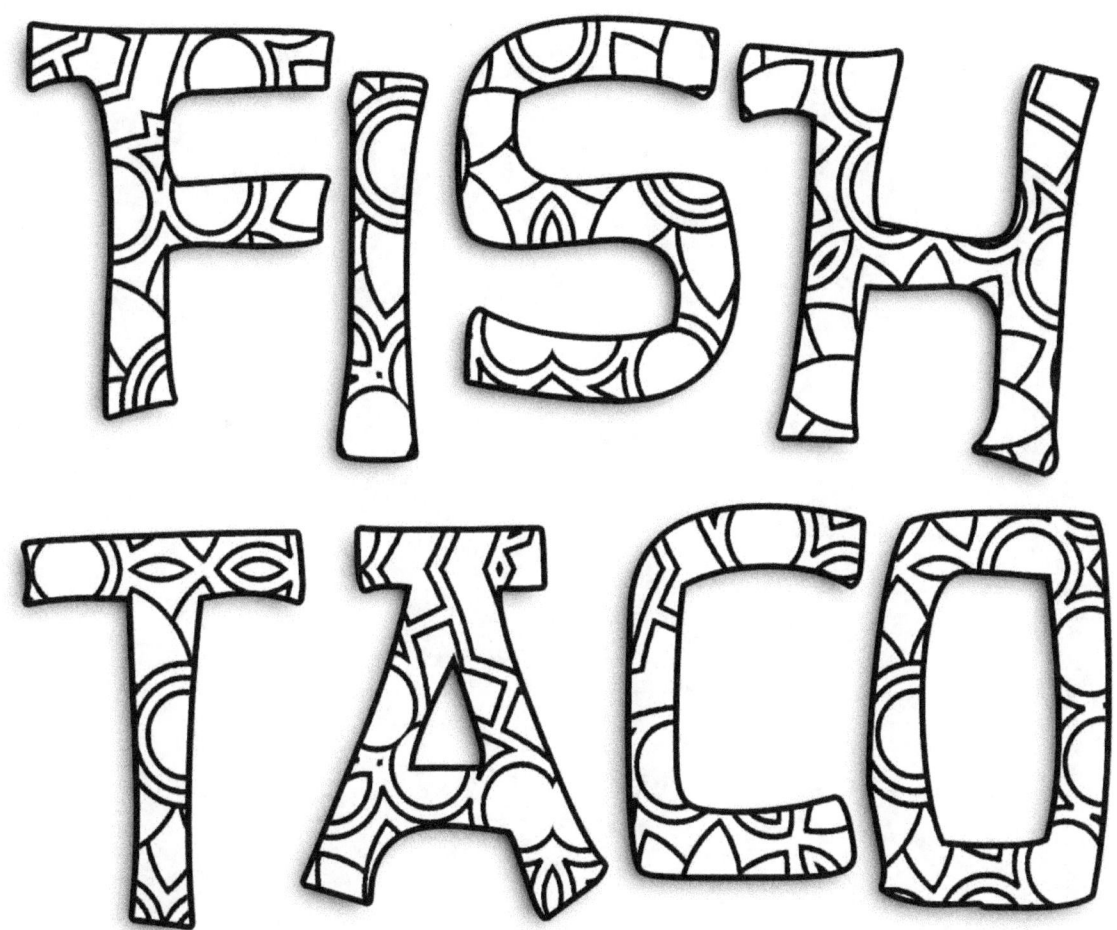

BUSHY
BEAVER

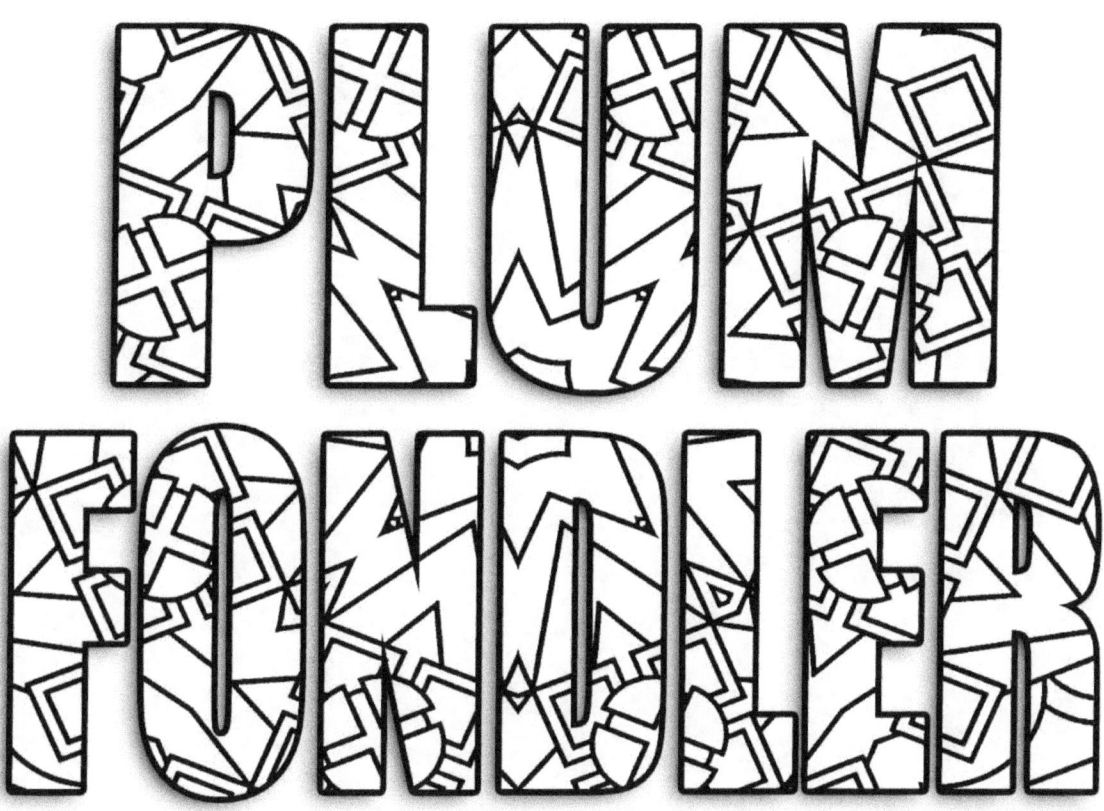

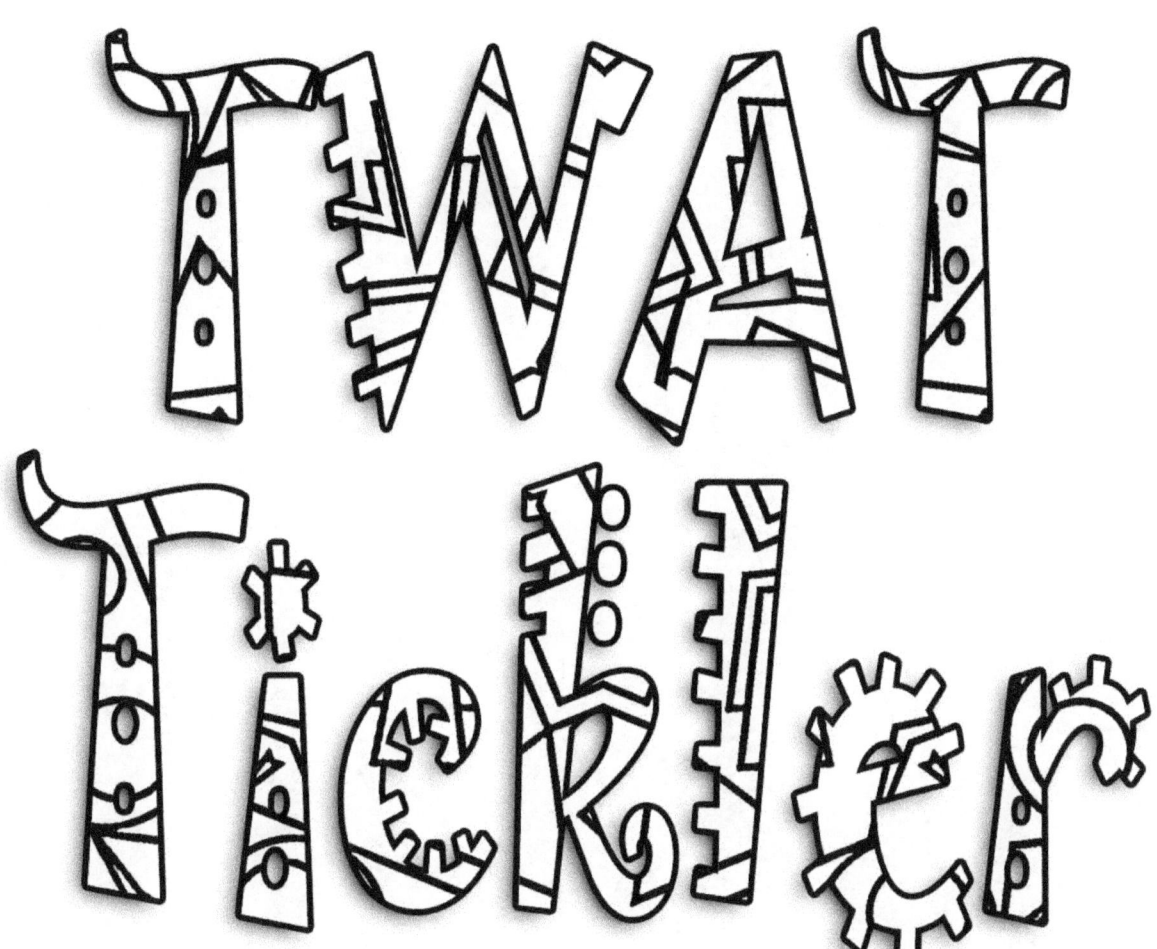

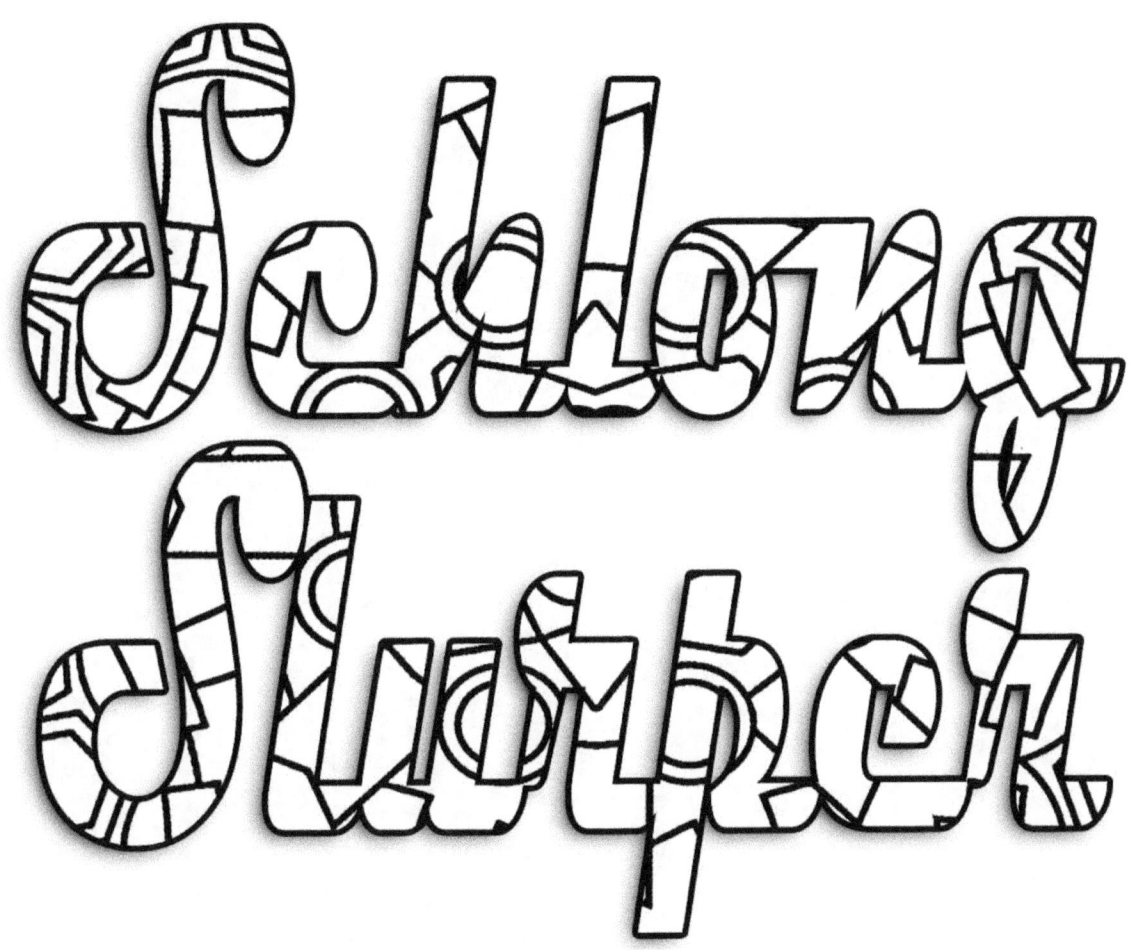

TURd

W1ZARd

CIRCLE SQUIRTER

Street
Walker

TRANNY TUGGER

Spaghetti Girth

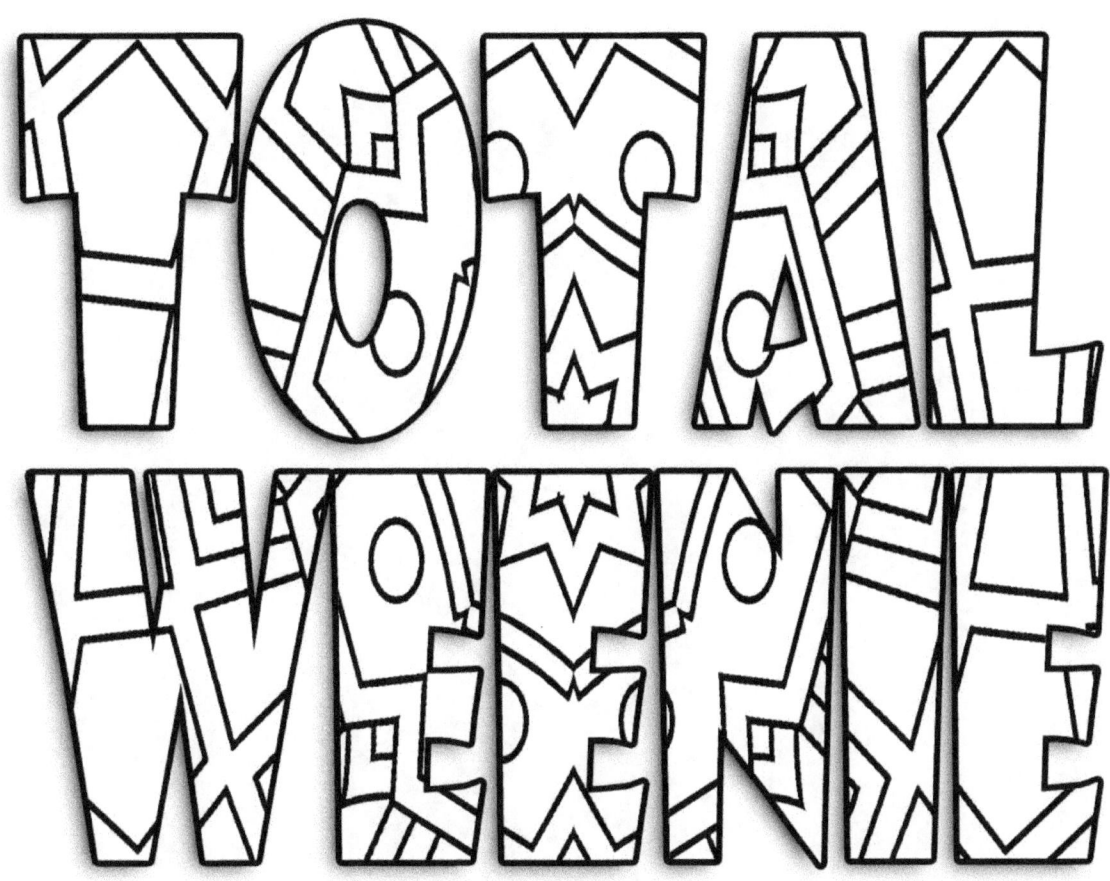

www.ingramcontent.com/pod-product-compliance
Lightning Source LLC
Chambersburg PA
CBHW080555190526
45169CB00007B/2780